Practice in the Basic Skills   English 2

Contents

Published by Collins Educational
An imprint of HarperCollins*Publishers* Ltd
77-85 Fulham Palace Road
London W6 8JB

www.CollinsEducation.com
On-line support for schools and colleges

© Derek Newton and David Smith 2003
First published 1978
This edition published 2003
Reprinted 12

ISBN-13 9780007177172

The authors assert the moral right to be identified as the authors of this work.

British Library Cataloguing in Publication Data
A catalogue record for this book is available from the British Library.

Illustrated by A Rodger

Printed by Martins the Printers, Berwick upon Tweed

The alphabet

```
a  b  c  d  e  f  g  h  i  j  k  l  m
n  o  p  q  r  s  t  u  v  w  x  y  z
```

1 What is the third letter?
2 Which letter comes after v?
3 Write the sixth letter.
4 Which is the last letter of all?
5 Write the letter that comes between n and p.
6 Write the two letters on either side of s.
7 Which letter comes before h?
8 Which letter is next but one before k?
9 Write the letter next but one before c.
10 What are the missing letters?

         c d _ f g h _ j k l m _ _ p

    f c e d a b   are jumbled letters

    a b c d e f   are in 'a b c' order

Write these in 'a b c' order.
1 d g c f e
2 r p t q s
3 j k i g h
4 x z v y w
5 f g c b e d
6 s v r q t p u

Alphabetical order

queen	jug	violin	camel	window	key	bell
egg	zebra	medal	sheep	axe	umbrella	igloo
goose	rocket	x-ray	fox	loaf	yak	pan	tap
nail	owl	dog	hammer			

Write these names in the same order as the twenty-six pictures. This means in alphabetical order.

1 _____ **2** _____ and so on.

Animal word puzzles

Put the letters under these twenty pictures in the right order to make the correct names of the animals.

1 tba	**2** rede	**3** lmcae	**4** mrwo
5 odta	**6** rbae	**7** galee	**8** barc
9 gaiferf	**10** oshre	**11** emlo	**12** menoyk
13 ospoutc	**14** tropar	**15** letrut	**16** malsno
17 emrhats	**18** tomh	**19** grolial	**20** croodclie

Who does what?

Write the correct name at the beginning of each of the ten sentences to match the pictures.

1 ___ is feeding her rabbits.
2 ___ is mending an engine.
3 ___ is kicking a football.
4 ___ is washing her hair.
5 ___ is speaking on the phone.
6 ___ is skateboarding.
7 ___ is painting the wall.
8 ___ is skating.
9 ___ is making a model.
10 ___ is riding a horse.

Find the best word

Choose a describing word from the list below to fit each picture.

1 an _____ table   2 a _____ window   3 a _____ boy
4 a _____ hill   5 a _____ knife   6 a _____ day
7 a _____ egg   8 a _____ tower   9 a _____ cushion
10 an _____ witch   11 a _____ day   12 a _____ animal
13 _____ fingers   14 a _____ girl   15 a _____ bag
16 a _____ road

happy   wet   tall   ugly   winding   broken   sharp
sticky   foggy   oblong   cracked   steep   heavy   sad
huge   round

Alphabetical order

```
a b c d e f g h i j k l m
n o p q r s t u v w x y z
```

Write out in alphabetical order.

1 Edwin   Bill   George   Alan   Clive   Hugh   Derek   Fred

2 Carol   Heather   Alison   Brenda   Edna   Denise
   Gwen   Fiona

3 grape   apple   melon   pear   banana   fig   orange
   lemon

4 Kevin   Rachel   Joy   Ian   Clare   Andrew   Wendy
   Paul   Val   Linda   Nigel   Tammy   Mark   Sandra
   Harry

5 Poland   England   Austria   Wales   Turkey   Canada
   Germany   Norway   Belgium   Kenya   Russia
   Scotland   Ireland   Japan   Denmark   Mexico

6 Wrexham   Birmingham   Torquay   Rangers   Leeds
   Arsenal   Mansfield   Glentoran   Newcastle   Hull
   Everton   Celtic

Sorting

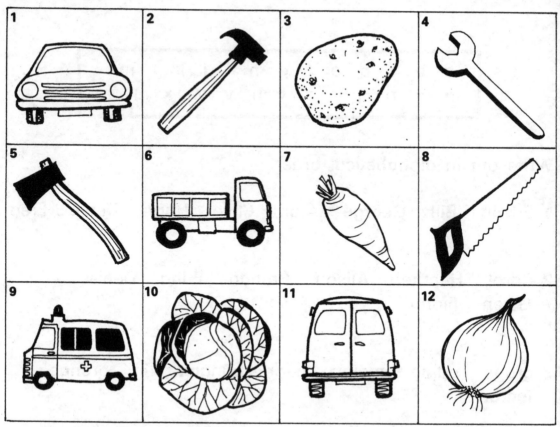

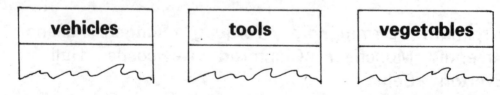

carrot   ambulance   spanner   car   saw   onion
hammer   lorry   potato   axe   cabbage   van

Write the correct name for each picture.

1 _____ 2 _____ and so on.
Now draw three boxes and label them.

Write the names of the objects in the correct boxes.

vehicles	tools	vegetables

Picture comprehension (1)

This list of words will help you to complete the six sentences.

Concorde	ship	spend	aeroplane	model	engine

1 Andrew has 50p to _____.

2 He goes in the _____ shop.

3 He looks at a large _____.

4 Next he looks at a _____.

5 He likes the _____.

6 At last he buys the _____.

# of or off

A Write **of** or **off** to complete the sentences.

1 May I buy two packets _____ crisps?
2 My hat was blown _____ by the wind.
3 Brian fell _____ his skateboard.
4 Have you heard _____ Jim Floyd lately?
5 One _____ the acrobat's tricks was diving _____ the pier.

to, too or two

B Write **to, too** or **two** to complete the sentences.

1 We saw _____ men climb the ladder.
2 Are you going _____ the cinema?
3 Pat is _____ old _____ join the Brownies.
4 Our dog is _____ fat _____ go on long walks.
5 _____ cars went _____ fast in the fog.

were or where

C Write **were** or **where** to complete the sentences.

1 _____ are you going for your holidays?
2 There _____ many ships in the docks.
3 I don't know _____ my dog is.
4 The children _____ very tired after swimming.
5 _____ do you think you _____ going last night?

Dictionary practice (1)

Use your dictionary to find the words that match these nine picture clues.

Each word begins with **t**.
The first two letters are given.

1 tr _ _ _ _

2 tu _ _ _ _ _

3 ti _ _ _ _

4 to _ _

5 to _ _ _ _

6 tr _ _ _ _ _ _

7 to _ _ _ _ _ _ _

8 ta _ _

9 te _ _ _ _ _ _ _

Choose the correct word

A Write out the name for each picture. The words below will help you.

```
aeroplane   boy   loaf   lion   cup   bus
cake   leaf   rabbit   flag   feather   house
```

B Here are twelve naming words.

```
clock   fire   hen   train   bicycle   kettle
ice   bell   chair   dolphin   moon   cow
```

Write the correct name of the object which

1 has two wheels.

2 lays eggs.

3 is cold.

4 shows the time.

5 lives in the sea.

6 shines at night.

7 boils water.

8 keeps you warm.

9 you sit on.

10 you ring.

11 gives milk.

12 travels on rails.

Picture comprehension (2)

The list of words will help you to complete the sentences.

1 Joy and ___ are playing with a ___.

2 Joy ___ the ball into the ___.

3 The ball ___ in the ___.

4 Tammy ___ her fishing ___.

5 Joy tries to ___ the ball ___ of the pond

6 She ___ and ___ into the water.

7 Joy is ___ and throws the ball on to the ___.

8 The ___ girls ran to their ___.

net	house	Tammy	water	grass	slips	ball	out
two	throws	brings	falls	drag	air	laughing	drops

Words with sh

A Write the correct name for each picture.

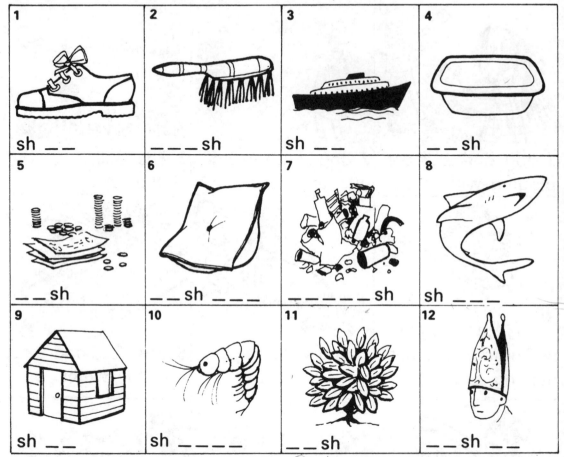

1 sh _ _	2 _ _ _ sh	3 sh _ _	4 _ _ sh
5 _ _ sh	6 _ _ sh _ _ _	7 _ _ _ _ _ _ sh	8 sh _ _ _
9 sh _ _	10 sh _ _ _ _	11 _ _ sh	12 _ _ sh _ _

B   Choose from this list.

1 The opposite of pull is	bush	push	hush
2 The opposite of deep is	sham	shall	shallow
3 The opposite of blunt is	shark	sharp	short
4 The opposite of open is	shout	shut	shirt
5 The opposite of start is	shop	finish	ship
6 The opposite of whisper is	shout	shift	short
7 The opposite of tall is	shut	short	shout
8 The opposite of stale is	flesh	fresh	hush

Where is it?

Look at the pictures.
Use a word from the list to complete each of the ten sentences.

1 The lion jumped ___ the hoop.
2 Sally hid ___ the hedge.
3 The boy fell ___ the river.
4 The gorilla is ___ his cage.
5 Ken and Roy walked ___ me.
6 The doctor stood ___ the bed.

7 The lady walked ___ the road.
8 The helicopter is ___ the houses.
9 The dog is ___ the chair.
10 The jockey is ___ the two horses.

| under | towards | above | beside | behind |
| between | through | across | into | outside |

Picture comprehension (3)

Write out the correct sentence to match each numbered picture.

The elephants are feeding.
The gorilla beats his chest.
Peter is going to the zoo.

He looks at the monkeys.
Peter watches the seals swim.
The parrot talks to Peter.

has or have

A Complete the sentences using **has** or **have**.

1 Neil _____ a new anorak today.
2 Dawn and Brenda _____ finished their work.
3 The astronauts _____ landed on the moon.
4 The giraffe _____ a very long neck.
5 _____ the rabbits been fed?

is or his

B Complete the sentences using **is** or **his**.

1 Skateboarding _____ great fun.
2 Tom often takes _____ dog for walks.
3 Derek lost _____ watch on the beach.
4 _____ that a Siamese cat?
5 When _____ Mark going to finish _____ book?

as or has

C Complete the sentences using **as** or **has**.

1 Carole _____ a new guitar.
2 Bill sang _____ he cleaned his bike.
3 Paul can run _____ fast _____ Danny.
4 Where _____ the caretaker put the mop?
5 Susan _____ grown _____ tall _____ Heather.

Mixed bag (1)

A The answers to these eight clues begin with the letters **tr**.

1 To do your best. tr _

2 A pony does this. tr _ _

3 You can carry things on one. tr _ _

4 Sometimes animals are caught in one. tr _ _

5 You are honest if you are this. tr _ _

6 Grows in a forest or wood or garden. tr _ _

7 A river fish. tr _ _ _

8 A musical instrument. tr _ _ _ _ _

B Write out the opposite of these words. Choose from this list.

> top   slow   fresh   day
> cold   wet   strong   short

1 night _____   5 long _____

2 weak _____   6 bottom _____

3 fast _____   7 dry _____

4 hot _____   8 stale _____

C Choose one of the words from the list below to fill each space.

1 ____ pencil 2 ____ hill   3 ____ day   4 ____ flower

5 ____ tail   6 ____ water 7 ____ story 8 ____ lion

> fierce   yellow   deep   steep
> sharp   exciting   rainy   bushy

Dictionary practice (2)

3 cl _ _ _

4 cr _ _

5 ch _ _ _

1 ca _ _ _

2 ca _ _

6 co _ _ _ _

7 ca _ _ _ _

8 co _ _

Use your dictionary to find the words that match these fourteen picture clues. Each word begins with **c**. The first two letters are given.

12 cu _ _ _ _ _ _

10 ca _ _ _ _

9 ch _ _ _ _ _

13 co _ _ _ _ _

11 cl _ _ _

14 cu _ _ _ _ _

ee and ea

Write the correct name for each picture. Remember each word
has either **ee** or **ea** in it.

1 b _ _	2 b _ _ _ _	3 s _ _ _ _	4 t _ _ _
5 w _ _ _ _	6 c _ _ _ _ _	7 s _ _	8 d _ _ _
9 l _ _ _	10 f _ _ _	11 h _ _ _	12 s _ _ _
13 b _ _ _	14 w _ _ _ _	15 m _ _ _	16 b _ _ _ _ _

Collections

Write the correct name for each picture. These words will help you.

flock	shoal	kit	pride	swarm	litter	library
bunch	pile	herd	bundle	forest	pack	choir

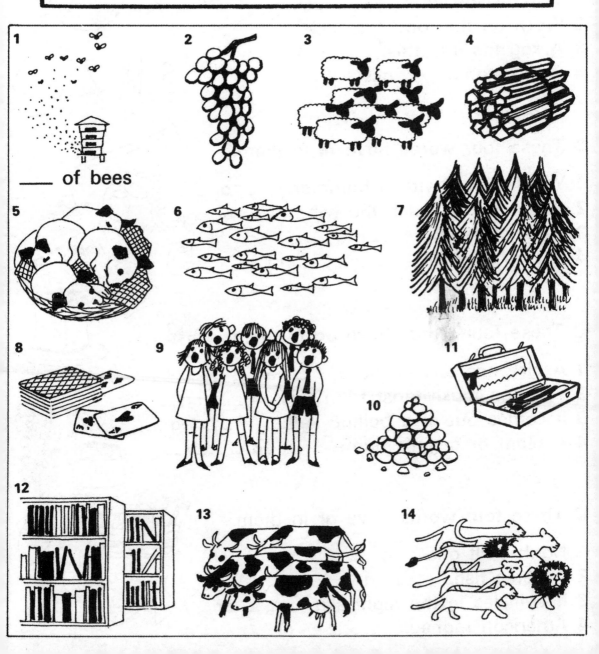

1

_____ of bees

2

3

4

5

6

7

8

9

10

11

12

13

14

Spelling (1)

The picture clues will help you.

A These four words end in **ock**.

1 Tells us the time. _ _ ock
2 Worn on the foot. _ ock
3 A key fits into this. _ ock
4 A big stone. _ ock

B These four words have **ai** in them.

1 You knock it with a hammer. _ ai _
2 On a ship to catch the wind. _ ai _
3 Links of metal. _ _ ai _
4 A very high hill. _ _ _ _ _ _ ai _

C These four words have **ea** in them.

1 A bird has one of these. _ ea _
2 You can make toast from this. _ _ ea _
3 It comes out of a boiling kettle. _ _ ea _
4 A plant or a girl's name. _ ea _ _ _ _ _

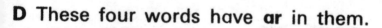

D These four words have **ar** in them.

1 Noah built one. ar _
2 A fierce fish. _ _ ar _
3 It twinkles in the night sky. _ _ ar
4 American money. _ _ _ _ ar

Dictionary practice (3)

4 sh _ _ _

2 sh _ _

1 sh _ _

5 se _ _

6 st _ _ _

3 st _ _ _ _ _

Use your dictionary to find
the words that match these
seventeen picture clues.

7 SW _ _

10 sp _ _ _ _

8 sn _ _ _ _ _ _

9 sn _ _ _

11 sq _ _ _ _ _ _

Each word begins with **s**.
The first two letters are given.

12 sp _ _ _ _ _

16 sn _ _ _

15 sh _ _ _

17 SU _ _ _ _ _ _ _

14 SW _ _ _

13 st _ _ _

there or their

A Complete these sentences using either **there** or **their**.

1 My house is _____.
2 Jim and Sue waved to _____ friend.
3 Derek and Mark lost _____ way.
4 I stayed _____ all day.
5 The girls showed me _____ presents.
6 _____ are 48 pages in this book.
7 Watch the blackbirds feed _____ young.
8 When I arrived _____ Malcolm had gone.

here or hear

B Complete these sentences using either **here** or **hear**.

1 Kim has come _____ to play with you.
2 Bob didn't _____ the whistle blow.
3 Mary was _____ yesterday.
4 Please wait _____ for me.
5 I can _____ you clearly.
6 Did you _____ your mother shout?
7 _____ is the book you lost.
8 Deaf people cannot _____.

Long o sound

There is a long **o** sound in each of the words that match the sixteen pictures.

Write the correct name for each picture.
1 boat **2** _____ and so on.

These words will help you.

phone	bow	soap	boat	hole	loaf	coat	window
cone	arrow	road	goat	snowman	bowl	hoe	bone

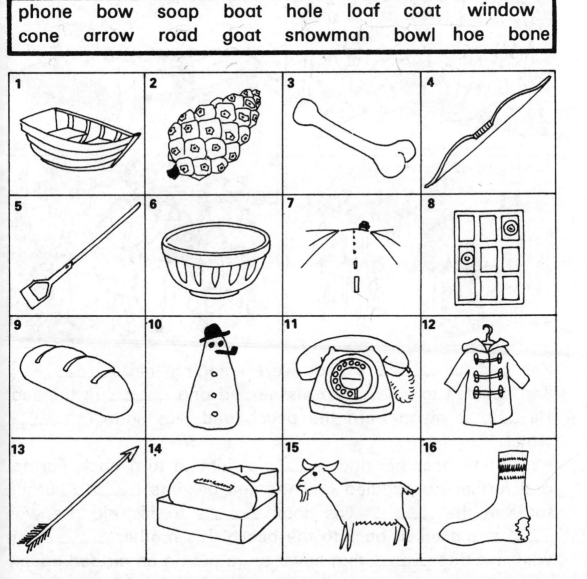

Picture comprehension (4)

Write out the story filling in the thirteen spaces by using words from this list.

rescued	deep	told	blow	three	shouting	speeding
holiday	lifeboat	dried	play	rough	paddled	

Ken and his _____ friends were enjoying their _____.
Ken decided to _____ up his air-bed and _____ in the sea.
He _____ away from the beach and was soon in _____ water.
Ken didn't hear his dad _____ at him to turn back. Further and further he paddled and the sea became _____. Luckily for Ken the _____ was soon _____ to his aid. He was _____ and taken back to the beach. His mother _____ him while his dad _____ him never to go out on an air-bed again.

Spelling (2)

The picture clues will help you.

A All these words end in **ey**.

1 Used to open locks. _ ey
2 Made by bees. _ _ _ ey
3 You earn it and spend it. _ _ _ ey
4 Like a small horse with big ears. _ _ _ _ _ ey

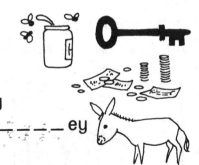

B All these words begin with **wh**.

1 A huge sea animal. wh _ _ _
2 A car should have a spare one. wh _ _ _
3 Flour is made from this. wh _ _ _
4 A cat has these. wh _ _ _ _ _ _

C All these words have **oa** in them.

1 A tree. oa _
2 A young horse. _ oa _
3 Cars and lorries travel on these. _ oa _ _
4 Water round a castle. _ oa _

D All these words end in **el**.

1 Home for a dog. _ _ _ _ el
2 Used for drying yourself. _ _ _ el
3 Seen on ships. _ _ _ _ el
4 An animal of the desert. _ _ _ el

Dictionary practice (4)

Use your dictionary to find the words that match these picture clues.

Each word begins with **w**.

The first two letters are given.

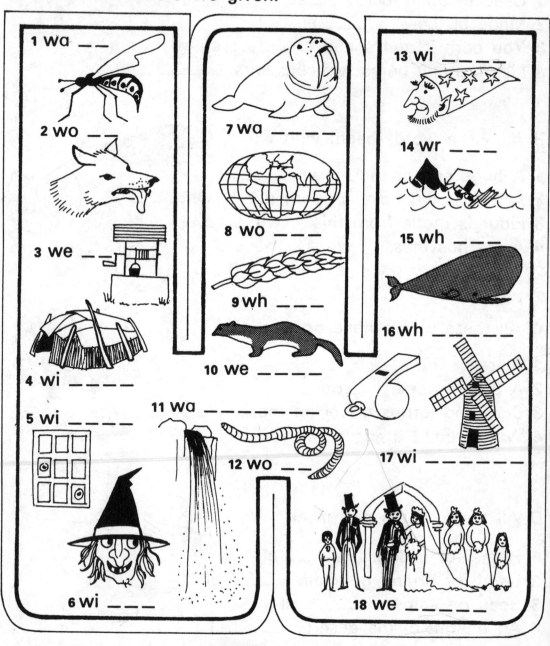

1 wa _ _ _

2 wo _ _ _

3 we _ _ _

4 wi _ _ _ _ _

5 wi _ _ _ _ _

6 wi _ _ _ _

7 wa _ _ _ _ _

8 wo _ _ _ _

9 wh _ _ _ _

10 we _ _ _ _ _

11 wa _ _ _ _ _ _ _ _

12 wo _ _ _

13 wi _ _ _ _ _ _

14 wr _ _ _ _

15 wh _ _ _ _

16 wh _ _ _ _ _

17 wi _ _ _ _ _ _ _

18 we _ _ _ _ _ _

Action words

Choose the right **action** word for each picture.

Write your sentences like this: **1** The wind blows.

These words will help you.

rolls	flies	falls	blows	swims	sails	crawls	bakes
rides	brushes	shines	flows	burns	runs	writes	drives

1. wind	**2** mother	**3** dinghy	**4** Sally
5 baby	**6** Pat	**7** rain	**8** sun
9 Tim	**10** dog	**11** fire	**12** aeroplane
13 wheel	**14** farmer	**15** fish	**16** river

Long i sound

There is a long **i** sound (say **eye**) in each of these words that match the sixteen pictures.

Write the correct name for each picture:
1 pipe   **2** _____ and so on.

These words will help you.

knife	miner	kite	guy	pile	mice	sky	pie	fly
slide	python	pipe	night	tiger	pilot	tie		

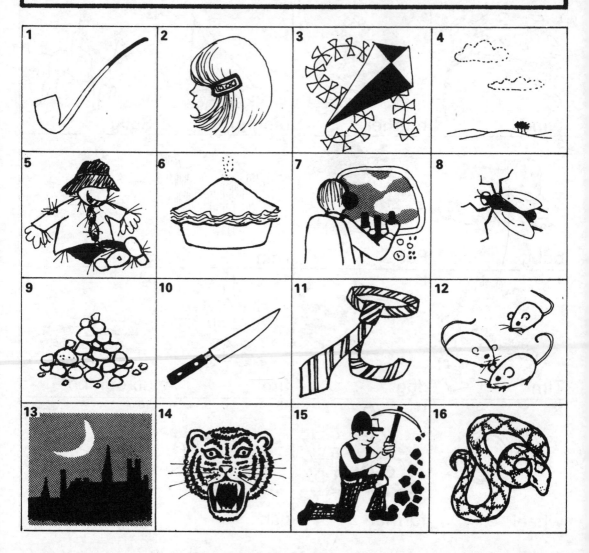

Picture comprehension (5)

Write out the story filling in the eleven spaces by choosing your own words.

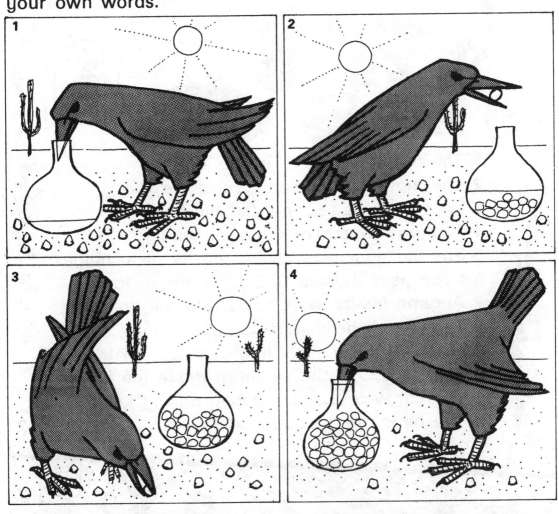

It is very hot in the _____. The sun beats down all day drying up any _____. A bird is very _____. Suddenly he sees a jar which _____ a little water. The mouth of the jar is too _____ and his _____ cannot reach the water. He is a clever bird and he has a good _____. He collects _____ and drops them, one by one, into the jar. The _____ of water rises until, at _____, the bird is able to _____.

Sound words

Choose the best sound words to complete the sentences.

1 The tap was _____ in the sink.
2 The monkeys were _____ in the zoo.
3 Bees were _____ around the hive.
4 Tammy's watch was _____ loudly.
5 The old door was _____ on its rusty hinges.
6 I can hear thunder _____ in the distance.
7 Autumn leaves were _____ in the breeze.
8 The church bells were _____.
9 Listen to the horse's hoofs _____ on the road.
10 The _____ of the car horn made me jump.
11 The cat was _____ happily on my knee.
12 The birds are _____ in the trees.

ticking   dripping   humming   creaking   ringing   purring
rumbling   chirping   rustling   tooting   chattering
clattering

Dictionary practice (5)

Use your dictionary to find the words that match these twelve picture clues.
Each word begins with **m**.
The first two letters are given.

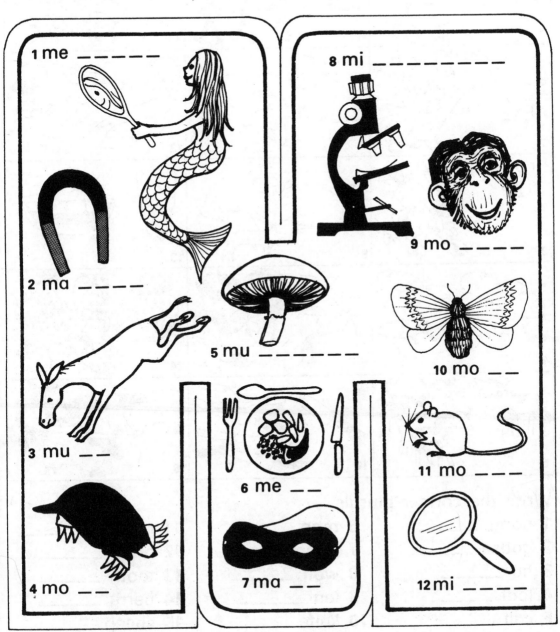

1 me _ _ _ _ _ _

2 ma _ _ _ _ _

3 mu _ _

4 mo _ _

5 mu _ _ _ _ _ _

6 me _ _

7 ma _ _

8 mi _ _ _ _ _ _ _ _

9 mo _ _ _ _

10 mo _ _

11 mo _ _ _ _

12 mi _ _ _ _

More than one

Here are fifteen pictures.

Write the correct plurals.

1 pony _____

2 goose _____

3 fly _____

4 loaf _____

5 calf _____

6 man _____

7 puppy _____

8 wolf _____

9 leaf _____

10 knife _____

11 mouse _____

12 baby _____

13 tooth _____

14 berry _____

15 sheep _____

Picture comprehension (6)

Read the sentence under each picture. Write another sentence telling what happened.

1. Pat was playing on the ice.
She _____

2. Tabby crept closer to the bird.
He _____

3. Colin was climbing a tree.
He _____

4. The sand castle was finished.
The _____

5. Mr. Clark ran to the bus stop.
The _____

6. Wendy fell off her bicycle.
She _____

7. Peter was fishing in the river.
He _____

8. Tim and Simon were playing football.
Mr. Ash _____

Mixed bag (2)

A Choose one of the words from the list to fill each space.

1 The clock _____.
2 The sun _____.
3 The telephone _____.
4 The footballer _____.

5 The owl _____.
6 The baby _____.
7 The soldier _____.
8 The dog _____.

> rings   hoots   ticks   barks   scores
> marches   crawls   shines

B Choose from the list the words which **rhyme** with the ten words below.

1 tail _____
2 heel _____
3 leak _____
4 farm _____
5 stoat _____

6 bird _____
7 wood _____
8 night _____
9 lane _____
10 neat _____

> week   word   gale   white   calm
> vote   peal   sheet   train   could

C Choose the correct words from the list to match male and female in the words below.

1 son _____
2 _____ girl
3 man _____

4 _____ she
5 nephew _____
6 _____ aunt

7 cock _____
8 _____ witch
9 bull _____

10 _____ doe

> niece   cow   woman   buck   daughter
> uncle   boy   hen   he   wizard

Who uses what?

Choose from the words to complete the fourteen sentences.

1 A nurse uses a _____.
2 A farmer uses a _____.
3 A fireman uses a _____.
4 A bricklayer uses a _____.
5 A sailor uses a _____.
6 An artist uses a _____.
7 A cook uses a _____.
8 A dentist uses a _____.
9 A joiner uses a _____.
10 A hairdresser uses _____.
11 A fisherman uses a _____.
12 A gardener uses a _____.
13 A mechanic uses a _____.
14 A conductor uses a _____.

| baton | thermometer | drill | rake | scissors | tractor | cooker |
| trowel | compass | palette | spanner | rod | saw | hose |

Joining sentences

A Use **and** to join these six pairs of sentences.

1 I went to the shop. I bought some sweets.
2 David ate his tea. David went to the cinema.
3 Jill sat down. She started to read a book.
4 We went to the zoo. We saw many animals.
5 Dad likes golf. Dad likes football.
6 A cow was in the field. A horse was in the field.

B Use **but** to join these six pairs of sentences.

1 An elephant is huge. A mouse is tiny.
2 A tortoise is slow. A cheetah is fast.
3 John went to the shop. The shop was closed.
4 Dad's car is new. Uncle's car is old.
5 Heather enjoys painting. Heather doesn't like sewing.
6 Mark wanted an ice cream. He had no money.

C Use **and** or **but** to join these six pairs of sentences.

1 We went to the circus. We saw the clowns.
2 Sally fell down. She was not hurt.
3 Snow is white. Coal is black.
4 Jed phoned Paul. Paul was not in.
5 Mr. Simm sat on his chair. He fell fast asleep.

Completing sentences

Here are the endings of ten sentences. Add words of your own to make interesting sentences. The pictures will help you.

1   and fell over.

2   but did not win.

3   and counted his money.

4   when her puppy ran off.

5   while his friends put up the tent.

6   and it flew away.

7   before the firemen came.

8   because of the deep snow.

9   but found nothing.

10   when the Queen came.

Similar words

These fifteen pairs of words are alike in meaning.

halt — stop	big — large	rich — wealthy
mend — repair	hard — difficult	rip — tear
end — finish	speak — talk	pull — tug
gift — present	begin — start	wide — broad
round — circular	sore — painful	goodbye — farewell

In place of each word in heavy type write the word which has a similar meaning.

1 Sometimes maths can be **hard**.
2 The film will **end** at ten o'clock.
3 The red traffic light means you must **stop**.
4 My ankle is **sore**.
5 The table is too **broad** to fit through the door.
6 If you **pull** hard, it will come out.
7 Thank you for your **gift**.
8 There is a **tear** in your skirt.
9 Do you like **round** tables?
10 The joiner will **repair** the door.
11 Never **speak** to strangers.
12 When will you **begin** to work harder?
13 The U.S.A. is a **rich** country.
14 I said **farewell** to our visitors.
15 Russia is a **big** country.

The spider

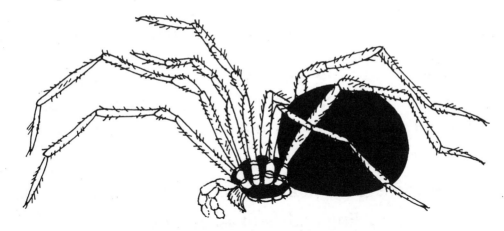

The spider's body is in two parts. An insect's body has three parts. Spiders have eight legs while insects have six legs.

Many spiders spin webs to catch insects. The spider hides in a silk tube and darts out on the insect trapped in the web. The insect is killed by the spider's poisonous bite.

The female spider lays her eggs in a cocoon or silk bag. The young hatch out as complete spiders in the spring.

None of the British spiders is harmful so you need not be frightened of them.

Answer these questions in sentences.

1 How many legs has a spider?
2 How many legs has an insect?
3 How many parts has an insect's body?
4 How many parts has a spider's body?
5 What does a spider spin?
6 Where does the spider hide?
7 How does a spider kill an insect?
8 In what does the female lay her eggs?
9 When do young spiders hatch out?

Mixed bag (3)

A Join each pair of words together. Remember the ' goes where the **o** was.

1 was not	**2** does not	**3** are not
4 do not	**5** is not	**6** have not
7 were not	**8** has not	**9** did not

B Complete these six sentences with **saw** or **seen**.

1 Paul _____ England beat Australia.

2 Have you _____ my dog?

3 I have _____ the Queen.

4 The boys _____ the Jumbo jet land.

5 Bill was _____ by the teacher.

6 I am sure the teacher _____ Bill.

C The names of the eight things you see in the pictures are made by joining two words together:

flower + pot ⟶ flowerpot

Use these two lists of words to help you.

foot	snow	light	sheep	butter	news	tea	black

+

dog	fly	man	paper	pot	bird	house	ball

Word building

A By writing the letter **p** before **rice** we make the word **price**. Write a letter before each of the eight words below to make the words match the clues.

1 _ ice	The cat caught two _____.
2 _ ash	I saw lots of _____ at the bank.
3 _ age	Who tore that _____?
4 _ air	You must have your _____ cut.
5 _ harp	Be careful! That knife is _____.
6 _ witch	_____ off the lights.
7 _ lower	The snowdrop is a pretty _____.
8 _ right	That noise gave me a _____.

B By writing the letters **wh** before **eel** we make the word **wheel**.
Write two letters before each of the eight words below to make the words match the clues.

1 _ _ raw	Get some _____ for the rabbits.
2 _ _ able	Take the horse to his _____.
3 _ _ actor	The farmer drives his _____.
4 th row	Paul can _____ a ball a long way.
5 st ride	A giant has a long _____.
6 st art	_____ when you are ready.
7 th rough	You can see _____ a window.
8 sp ill	I hope you don't _____ any milk.

Punctuation

A Write out the twelve words in this list which should begin with a **capital letter**.

> boy   tree   peter   carrot   glasgow   smith
> hen   monday   jones   ball   shop   japan
> cheshire   farmer   ann   blackpool   dog   car
> december   england   spoon   thursday   house
> pencil   cate

B There are two things to correct in each of the following sentences.

The mistakes could be full stops, question marks or capital letters.

1 did you know that I can swim

2 Derek and david live in manchester.

3 i'll see you in regent Street.

4 Simon watched Liverpool beat newcastle

5 cumbria and powys are counties of Britain.

6 I am playing football with paul and Mark

7 Does the thames flow through London

8 heather Smith lives at 12 beechways, Stirling.

9 We saw george the giraffe feeding at bristol Zoo.

10 Can you see Rod thomas running to school

Toucans

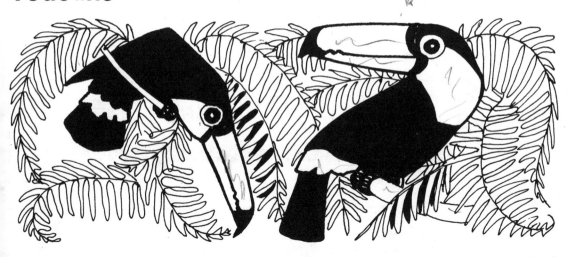

Most toucans live in the rain forests of the River Amazon. Toucans have a very large and brightly-coloured bill. Even though it is so large the toucan's bill is light in weight. This is because of the air spaces between the bill's thin, bony sides.

Toucans have a very long tongue. They feed mostly on fruits but they also eat insects, small reptiles and the eggs and chicks of small birds. Their long bills are very useful for plucking and crushing the food before it is swallowed.

Toucans lay their eggs in holes in trees.

Answer these questions in sentences.

1 Near which river do most toucans live?
2 In which kind of forests do the toucans live?
3 Which part of the toucan is very long?
4 Which part of the bird is very large and brightly-coloured?
5 What is the bill made of?
6 Why is the toucan's bill so light?
7 Where does the toucan lay its eggs?
8 What does a toucan eat?
9 Write down two uses of a toucan's bill.

Days, weeks and months

A

1 Write out the names of the days of the week.
2 Write out the names of the months of the year.
3 In what month is your birthday?
4 Which days of the week do we not come to school?
5 In what month does Christmas come?
6 In what month or months do we have our longest school holiday?
7 Which month has the fewest number of days?
8 In which month is the longest day?
9 In which month is the shortest day?

B Write the date for each of the following:

1 your birthday
2 New Year's Day
3 Hallowe'en
4 Boxing Day
5 Bonfire Night
6 today
7 St. David's Day
8 Remembrance Day
9 St. George's Day
10 your mum's birthday
11 St. Andrew's Day
12 your dad's birthday
13 St. Patrick's Day
14 your friend's birthday

Similar sounding words

A Choose the correct word from the brackets to complete the sentences.

1 I am going to _____ a present for mum. (by, buy)

2 Heather _____ a dress for her party. (made, maid)

3 Sally wore her _____ shoes. (knew, new)

4 The _____ looked very calm. (sea, see)

5 Kim did _____ win her race. (knot, not)

6 We lost _____ way in the fog. (our, hour)

7 Janet _____ her way to the zoo. (new, knew)

8 The _____ rises in the east. (son, sun)

9 The _____ has long ears and a short tail. (hair, hare)

10 Tim was _____ after his illness. (weak, week)

B Complete the sentences using the words given in brackets.

1 The footballer's sore _____ began to _____ slowly. (heal, heel)

2 The cyclist _____ quickly along the narrow _____. (road, rode)

3 It will take you an _____ to reach _____ house. (our, hour)

4 Darren _____ the ball _____ the window. (through, threw)

5 Do _____ tie the _____ too tight. (not, knot)

Verbs — past and present

A Change the word in bold type in each sentence to show that these things have already happened.

Present	Past
1 I **come** home.	I _____ home.
2 I **fly** to London.	I _____ to London.
3 I **see** the ship.	I _____ the ship.
4 I **paint** a picture.	I _____ a picture.
5 I **sing** songs.	I _____ songs.
6 Jane **hides** the present.	Jane _____ the present.
7 A dog **bites** Kim.	A dog _____ Kim.
8 I **drink** milk.	I _____ milk.
9 Susan **falls** down.	Susan _____ down.
10 Paul **does** his best work.	Paul _____ his best work.

B Change the word in bold type to show that these things are happening now.

Past	Present
1 I **gave** a present.	I _____ a present.
2 I **began** my work.	I _____ my work.
3 I **ate** my dinner.	I _____ my dinner.
4 I **drew** a picture.	I _____ a picture.
5 I **spoke** to him.	I _____ to him.
6 I **swam** in the pool.	I _____ in the pool.
7 I **dug** the garden.	I _____ the garden.
8 I **bought** some sweets.	I _____ some sweets.
9 I **ran** home.	I _____ home.
10 I **threw** the ball.	I _____ the ball.

Answers

Page 2 The alphabet
1 c 2 w 3 f 4 z 5 o 6 r, t 7 g 8 m 9 a 10 e, i, n, o
1 cdefg 2 pqrst 3 ghijk 4 vwxyz 5 bcdefg 6 pqrstuv

Page 3 Alphabetical order
1 axe 2 bell 3 camel 4 dog 5 egg 6 fox 7 goose
8 hammer 9 igloo 10 jug 11 key 12 loaf 13 medal
14 nail 15 owl 16 pan 17 queen 18 rocket 19 sheep
20 tap 21 umbrella 22 violin 23 window 24 x-ray
25 yak 26 zebra

Page 4 Animal word puzzles
1 bat 2 deer 3 camel 4 worm 5 toad 6 bear 7 eagle
8 crab 9 giraffe 10 horse 11 mole 12 monkey
13 octopus 14 parrot 15 turtle 16 salmon
17 hamster 18 moth 19 gorilla 20 crocodile

Page 5 Who does what?
1 Wendy 2 David 3 Mark 4 Emma 5 Heather 6 Paul
7 Edwin 8 Caroline 9 Derek 10 Judy

Page 6 Find the best word
1 oblong 2 broken 3 happy 4 steep 5 sharp 6 foggy
7 cracked 8 tall 9 round 10 ugly 11 wet 12 huge
13 sticky 14 sad 15 heavy 16 winding

Page 7 Alphabetical order
1 Alan, Bill, Clive, Derek, Edwin, Fred, George, Hugh
2 Alison, Brenda, Carol, Denise, Edna, Fiona, Gwen,
Heather
3 apple, banana, fig, grape, lemon, melon, orange, pear
4 Andrew, Clare, Harry, Ian, Joy, Kevin, Linda, Mark,
Nigel, Paul, Rachel, Sandra, Tammy, Val, Wendy
5 Austria, Belgium, Canada, Denmark, England,
Germany, Ireland, Japan, Kenya, Mexico, Norway,
Poland, Russia, Scotland, Turkey, Wales
6 Arsenal, Birmingham, Celtic, Everton, Glentoran,
Hull, Leeds, Mansfield, Newcastle, Rangers, Torquay,
Wrexham

Page 8 Sorting
1 car 2 hammer 3 potato 4 spanner 5 axe 6 lorry
7 carrot 8 saw 9 ambulance 10 cabbage 11 van
12 onion
vehicles car, lorry, ambulance, van
tools hammer, axe, spanner, saw
vegetables potato, carrot, onion, cabbage

Page 9 Picture comprehension (1)
1 spend 2 model 3 Concorde 4 ship 5 engine
6 aeroplane

Page 10 of or off
A 1 of 2 off 3 off 4 of 5 of, off

to, too or two
B 1 two 2 to 3 too, to 4 too, to 5 Two, too

were or where
C 1 Where 2 were 3 where 4 were 5 Where, were

Page 11 Dictionary practice (1)
1 tramp 2 tunnel 3 tiger 4 toad 5 tower 6 trumpet
7 tortoise 8 taxi 9 telephone

Page 12 Choose the correct word
A 1 loaf 2 bus 3 flag 4 cake 5 aeroplane 6 cup
7 feather 8 rabbit 9 leaf 10 lion 11 house 12 boy
B 1 bicycle 2 hen 3 ice 4 clock 5 dolphin 6 moon
7 kettle 8 fire 9 chair 10 bell 11 cow 12 train

Page 13 Picture comprehension (2)
1 Tammy, ball 2 throws, air 3 drops, water 4 brings,
net 5 drag, out 6 slips, falls 7 laughing, grass
8 two, house

Page 14 Words with sh
A 1 shoe 2 brush 3 ship 4 dish 5 cash 6 cushion
7 rubbish 8 shark 9 shed 10 shrimp 11 bush
12 bishop
B 1 push 2 shallow 3 sharp 4 shut 5 finish
6 shout 7 short 8 fresh

Page 15 Where is it?

1 through 2 behind 3 into 4 outside 5 towards
6 beside 7 across 8 above 9 under 10 between

Page 16 Picture comprehension (3)

1 Peter is going to the zoo. 2 He looks at the
monkeys. 3 The parrot talks to Peter. 4 The gorilla
beats his chest. 5 The elephants are feeding. 6 Peter
watches the seals swim.

Page 17 has or have

A 1 has 2 have 3 have 4 has 5 Have

is or his

B 1 is 2 his 3 his 4 Is 5 is, his

as or has

C 1 has 2 as 3 as, as 4 has 5 has, as, as

Page 18 Mixed bag (1)

A 1 try 2 trot 3 tray 4 trap 5 true 6 tree 7 trout
8 trumpet
B 1 day 2 strong 3 slow 4 cold 5 short 6 top 7 wet
8 fresh
C 1 sharp 2 steep 3 rainy 4 yellow 5 bushy 6 deep
7 exciting 8 fierce

Page 19 Dictionary practice (2)

1 camel 2 cake 3 clock 4 crab 5 chair 6 cowboy
7 camera 8 comb 9 chicken 10 cactus 11 clown
12 cucumber 13 compass 14 cupboard

Page 20 ee and ea

1 bee 2 beach 3 sheep 4 team 5 wheat 6 cheese
7 sea 8 deer 9 leaf 10 feet 11 heap 12 seat 13 bean
14 wheel -15 meal 16 beetle

Page 21 Collections

1 swarm 2 bunch 3 flock 4 bundle 5 litter 6 shoal
7 forest 8 pack 9 choir 10 pile 11 kit 12 library
13 herd 14 pride

Page 22 Spelling (1)
A 1 clock **2** sock **3** lock **4** rock
B 1 nail **2** sail **3** chain **4** mountain
C 1 beak **2** bread **3** steam **4** heather
D 1 ark **2** shark **3** star **4** dollar

Page 23 Dictionary practice (3)
1 shoe **2** shed **3** steeple **4** shark **5** seal **6** stool
7 swan **8** snowman **9** snail **10** spider **11** squirrel
12 sparrow **13** stork **14** sword **15** sheep **16** snake
17 submarine

Page 24 there or their
A 1 there **2** their **3** their **4** there **5** their **6** There
7 their **8** there

here or hear
B 1 here **2** hear **3** here **4** here **5** hear **6** hear **7** Here
8 hear

Page 25 Long o sound
1 boat **2** cone **3** bone **4** bow **5** hoe **6** bowl **7** road
8 window **9** loaf **10** snowman **11** telephone **12** coat
13 arrow **14** soap **15** goat **16** hole

Page 26 Picture comprehension (4)
1 three **2** holiday **3** blow **4** play **5** paddled **6** deep
7 shouting **8** rough **9** lifeboat **10** speeding
11 rescued **12** dried **13** told

Page 27 Spelling (2)
A 1 key **2** honey **3** money **4** donkey
B 1 whale **2** wheel **3** wheat **4** whiskers
C 1 oak **2** foal **3** roads **4** moat
D 1 kennel **2** towel **3** funnel **4** camel

Page 28 Dictionary practice (4)
1 wasp **2** wolf **3** well **4** wigwam **5** window **6** witch
7 walrus **8** world **9** wheat **10** weasel **11** waterfall
12 worm **13** wizard **14** wreck **15** whale **16** whistle
17 windmill **18** wedding

Page 29 Action words
1 blows 2 bakes 3 sails 4 rides 5 crawls 6 writes
7 falls 8 shines 9 brushes 10 runs 11 burns 12 flies
13 rolls 14 drives 15 swims 16 flows

Page 30 Long i sound
1 pipe 2 slide 3 kite 4 sky 5 guy 6 pie 7 pilot 8 fly
9 pile 10 knife 11 tie 12 mice 13 night 14 tiger
15 miner 16 python

Page 31 Picture comprehension (5)
desert, water/moisture, thirsty, contains/has, small,
beak, idea, stones/pebbles, level, last, drink

Page 32 Sound words
1 dripping 2 chattering 3 humming 4 ticking
5 creaking 6 rumbling 7 rustling 8 ringing
9 clattering 10 tooting 11 purring 12 chirping

Page 33 Dictionary practice (5)
1 mermaid 2 magnet 3 mule 4 mole 5 mushroom
6 meal 7 mask 8 microscope 9 monkey 10 moth
11 mouse 12 mirror

Page 34 More than one
1 ponies 2 geese 3 flies 4 loaves 5 calves 6 men
7 puppies 8 wolves 9 leaves 10 knives 11 mice
12 babies 13 teeth 14 berries 15 sheep

Page 35 Picture comprehension (6)
Check your child's sentences.

Page 36 Mixed bag (2)
A 1 ticks 2 shines 3 rings 4 scores 5 hoots 6 crawls
7 marches 8 barks
B 1 gale 2 peal 3 week 4 calm 5 vote 6 word
7 could 8 white 9 train 10 sheet
C 1 daughter 2 boy 3 woman 4 he 5 niece 6 uncle
7 hen 8 wizard 9 cow 10 buck

Page 37 Who uses what?
1 thermometer **2** tractor **3** hose **4** trowel **5** compass
6 palette **7** cooker **8** drill **9** saw **10** scissors **11** rod
12 rake **13** spanner **14** baton

Page 38 Joining sentences
A 1 I went to the shops and bought some sweets.
2 David ate his tea and went to the cinema.
3 Jill sat down and started to read a book.
4 We went to the zoo and saw many animals.
5 Dad likes golf and football.
6 A cow and a horse were in the field.

B 1 An elephant is huge but a mouse is tiny.
2 A tortoise is slow but a cheetah is fast.
3 John went to the shop but it was closed.
4 Dad's car is new but Uncle's car is old.
5 Heather enjoys painting but she doesn't like sewing.
6 Mark wanted an ice cream but he had no money.

C 1 We went to the circus and saw the clowns.
2 Sally fell down but she was not hurt.
3 Snow is white but coal is black.
4 Jed phoned Paul but Paul was not in.
5 Mr. Simm sat on his chair and fell fast asleep.

Page 39 Completing sentences
Check your child's sentences.

Page 40 Similar words
1 difficult **2** finish **3** halt **4** painful **5** wide **6** tug
7 present **8** rip **9** circular **10** mend **11** talk **12** start
13 wealthy **14** goodbye **15** large

Page 41 The spider
1 A spider has eight legs. **2** An insect has six legs.
3 An insect's body has three parts. **4** A spider's body
has two parts. **5** A spider spins webs. **6** A spider
hides in a silk tube. **7** A spider kills an insect with its
poisonous bite. **8** A female lays her eggs in a cocoon
or silk bag. **9** Young spiders hatch out in the spring.

Page 42 Mixed bag (3)

A 1 wasn't 2 doesn't 3 aren't 4 don't 5 isn't
6 haven't 7 weren't 8 hasn't 9 didn't
B 1 saw 2 seen 3 seen 4 saw 5 seen 6 saw
C 1 sheepdog 2 teapot 3 snowman 4 blackbird
5 football 6 lighthouse 7 newspaper 8 butterfly

Page 43 Word building

A 1 mice 2 cash 3 page 4 hair 5 sharp 6 switch
7 flower 8 fright
B 1 straw 2 stable 3 tractor 4 throw 5 stride 6 start
7 through 8 spill

Page 44 Punctuation

A Peter, Glasgow, Smith, Monday, Jones, Japan,
Cheshire, Blackpool, Ann, December, England,
Thursday
B 1 Did you know that I can swim?
2 Derek and David live in Manchester.
3 I'll see you in Regent Street.
4 Simon watched Liverpool beat Newcastle.
5 Cumbria and Powys are counties of Britain.
6 I am playing football with Paul and Mark.
7 Does the Thames flow through London?
8 Heather Smith lives at 12 Beechways, Stirling.
9 We saw George the giraffe feeding at Bristol Zoo.
10 Can you see Rod Thomas running to school?

Page 45 Toucans

1 Toucans live near the River Amazon. 2 Toucans
live in rain forests. 3 A toucan's tongue is very long.
4 A toucan's bill is very large and brightly-coloured.
5 The bill is made of bone. 6 A toucan's bill is so light
because of air spaces. 7 The toucan lays its eggs in
holes in the trees. 8 A toucan eats fruits, insects,
small reptiles and the eggs and chicks of small birds.
9 The toucan's bill is used for plucking and crushing
food.

Page 46 Days, weeks and months

A 1 Monday, Tuesday, Wednesday, Thursday, Friday, Saturday, Sunday

2 January, February, March, April, May, June, July, August, September, October, November, December

3 Check your child's answer.

4 Saturday and Sunday

5 December

6 July, August and September

7 February

8 June

9 December

B 1 Check your child's answer.

2 1st January

3 31st October

4 26th December

5 5th November

6 Check your child's answer.

7 1st March

8 11th November

9 23rd April

10 Check your child's answer.

11 30th November

12 Check your child's answer.

13 17th March

14 Check your child's answer.

Page 47 Similar sounding words

A 1 buy **2** made **3** new **4** sea **5** not **6** our **7** knew
8 sun **9** hare **10** weak

B 1 heel, heal **2** rode, road **3** hour, our **4** threw, through **5** not, knot

Page 48 Verbs past and present

A 1 came **2** flew **3** saw **4** painted **5** sang **6** hid **7** bit
8 drank **9** fell **10** did

B 1 give **2** begin **3** eat **4** draw **5** speak **6** swim
7 dig **8** buy **9** run **10** throw